Be It! Act It!

An Alphabet of Positive Emotions and Feelings

Little C Books

Corbett Shwom

Note to Parents and Caregivers

This book is your child's guide to exploring emotions that build bravery, confidence, and emotional strength while nurturing a positive mindset and emotional well-being. While some emotions may overlap, each is presented uniquely to deepen understanding and encourage children to embrace their feelings. By showing how actions can shape emotions, we empower children to actively engage in positive behaviors that foster happiness and resilience.

Published by Worry House Press
First Edition
Printed in the United States of America

www.corbettshwom.com

To all the amazing kids out there, this book is for you. Life is full of ups and downs, and it's okay to feel scared or unsure sometimes. Even when things seem tough, you are stronger and braver than you know. Remember, you are what you think. Believe in your strength and resilience. Let this book be a reminder of your courage and the power of positivity!

Hi, I'm Little C, your friendly guide through the alphabet of positive emotions and feelings! You might recognize me from the other Little C books.

With me by your side, you're about to go on a fun journey to explore the power of positive emotions and feelings. Did you know that by acting out these emotions, you can actually feel them too? Imagine feeling happy just by smiling! Go ahead, try it now. 😊 See how it works!

But first, let's talk about what *emotions* and *feelings* are. **Emotions** are things like happiness or sadness. **Feelings** are how we experience these emotions in our bodies and minds. For example, we smile when we're happy and cry when we're sad.

So, you're wondering if you can really become a certain positive emotion just by acting it out? You bet! If you want to **be** confident, **act** confident. It's like magic! But remember, just like learning any new skill, the more you practice, the better you'll get!

Are you ready? Turn the page and join me in discovering how to be, positive emotions from A to Z.

A is for Affectionate

If you want to **be** affectionate, **act** affectionate.

Give hugs, share kind words, and show love to those around you. Being affectionate means helping others feel warm and cared for.

B is for Brave

If you want to **be** brave, **act** brave.

Speak up, try new things, help others, and stand tall. Being brave means facing your fears while being smart and safe. Every brave act makes you stronger!

C is for Confident

If you want to **be** confident, **act** confident.

Do your homework, practice, walk tall, and make eye contact. Being confident means believing in yourself because you've prepared. It's knowing you can do well without being scared.

D is for Determined

If you want to **be** determined, **act** determined.

Set goals, work hard, and never give up, even when things get tough. Being determined means you keep trying, and with each step you get closer to your dreams.

E is for Empathetic

If you want to **be** empathetic, **act** empathetic.

Listen to others, understand their feelings, and offer support when they need it. Being empathetic means you know how others feel, making you kinder and a better friend.

F is for Forgiving

If you want to **be** forgiving, **act** forgiving.

Talk calmly, understand others, let go of bad feelings, and give second chances. Being forgiving means letting go of hurt and giving others the opportunity to make things right.

G is for Grateful

If you want to **be** grateful, **act** grateful.

Say "thank you," appreciate the people around you, and cherish the things that make you happy. Being grateful means you remember to value the good things in your life.

H is for Happy

If you want to **be** happy, **act** happy.

Smile, laugh, play, and enjoy every moment. Being happy means filling your heart with warm, good feelings. Happiness makes everything seem a little brighter.

I is for Inspired

If you want to **be** inspired, **act** inspired.

Whether it's drawing, writing, or exploring, let your imagination soar. Being inspired means feeling excited and creative. Inspiration is everywhere, just waiting to be found!

J is for Joyful

If you want to **be** joyful, **act** joyful.

Play, laugh, and enjoy the simple things that make you happy. Being joyful means finding happiness in everyday moments and sharing that joy with others.

K is for Kind

If you want to **be** kind, **act** kind.

Be caring, lend a helping hand, and treat others with respect.
Being kind means not only making others feel good but also
making yourself feel good too.

L is for Loving

If you want to **be** loving, **act** loving.

Show love with hugs, kind words, and simple acts of caring, like sharing or helping. Being loving means making friendships stronger and feeling closer to others.

M is for Mindful

If you want to **be** mindful, **act** mindful.

Take deep breaths, notice your surroundings, and focus on the present moment. Being mindful means you stay calm, focused, and appreciate the beauty around you.

N is for Nurturing

If you want to **be** nurturing, **act** nurturing.

Water plants, show kindness to animals, and help friends when they need it. Being nurturing means taking care of living things and helping them grow.

O is for Optimistic

If you want to **be** optimistic, **act** optimistic.

See the good in every situation, believe that good things can happen, and stay hopeful. Being optimistic means focusing on the positive, even when things are difficult.

P is for Peaceful

If you want to **be** peaceful, **act** peaceful.

Take deep breaths, find quiet moments, and let go of worries. Being peaceful means you feel calm and relaxed, making it easier to get along with others.

Q is for Quirky

If you want to **be** quirky, **act** quirky.

Celebrate your uniqueness, be silly, be different, and let your personality shine bright. Being quirky means adding color and laughter to the world, making life more fun and interesting.

R is for Resilient

If you want to **be** resilient, **act** resilient.

Keep trying, believe in yourself, and overcome challenges.
Being resilient means bouncing back from tough times and
growing stronger with each attempt.

S is for Strong

If you want to **be** strong, **act** strong.

Stand tall, believe in yourself, and face challenges with courage. Being strong means finding the strength inside you to get through hard times and reach your dreams.

T is for Thankful

If you want to **be** thankful, **act** thankful.

Show appreciation for people and things, and find happiness in little moments. Being thankful means recognizing what you have and sharing that feeling with others.

U is for Unwavering

If you want to **be** unwavering, **act** unwavering.

Hold on to your dreams, even when things get tough. Stay strong and keep going, no matter what. Being unwavering means sticking to your goals and never giving up.

V is for Valiant

If you want to **be** valiant, **act** valiant.

Face challenges with courage, stand up for others, and always do what is right. Being valiant means being brave and inspiring others to do the same, making the world a better place.

W is for Wise

If you want to **be** wise, **act** wise.

Seek knowledge, ask questions, and learn from your experiences. Being wise means making smart choices and understanding what life teaches you.

X is for eXtraordinary

If you want to **be** eXtraordinary, **act** eXtraordinary.

Dream big, use your talents, and make a difference in the world. Being eXtraordinary means believing in yourself and doing your best!

Y is for You

If you want to **be** you, **act** you.

Celebrate who you are and all the wonderful things that make you unique. You are one-of-a-kind, and the world is lucky to have you in it!

Z is for Zealous

If you want to **be** zealous, **act** zealous.

Put your heart into what you love. Have fun and be full of energy. Being zealous means doing things with excitement and enthusiasm, which helps you reach your goals.

Author's Note

Thank you for joining Little C on his journey through positive emotions and feelings! Remember, no matter what happens, you can change how you feel by what you do and how you act. Believe in yourself, act strong, act brave, act confident, just like Little C!

As you explore emotions like being brave, resilient, strong, and valiant, always make safe and smart choices. Acting these emotions means facing new challenges responsibly and safely. Remember this as you continue to grow and learn. ♥

Other Titles by Corbett Shwom

Worry Thoughts
A Story to Help Children Manage Worries and Anxious Thoughts

Worry Habits
A Story to Help Children Better Understand and Manage OCD

Worry Shy
A Story to Help Children Better Understand and Manage Social Anxiety

Newsletter

Get notified about Little C updates and new book releases.

https://corbettshwom.com

www.ingramcontent.com/pod-product-compliance
Lightning Source LLC
Chambersburg PA
CBHW041550040426
42447CB00002B/123